To Will One Thing

"Thy Kingdom Come,
Thy Will be done on Ec[...]"

Edited by
William Scarlett
Bishop of Missouri
1933-1952

revised and adapted by Almus Thorp

Forward Movement Publications
Cincinnati

This collection of prayers, hymns and quotations was first published by Christ Church Cathedral, St. Louis, Missouri, in 1948 and reissued in 1972. Forward Movement Publications is grateful to the Rev. Almus Thorp, retired Dean of Bexley Hall Divinity School, for selecting, editing and adapting these prayers for contemporary use.

revised edition

©1994, Forward Movement Publications, 412 Sycamore Street, Cincinnati, Ohio 45202 USA.

Contents

This collection of prayers, gathered from various sources, has long been in use in this Diocese, especially at Clergy Conferences, Quiet Hours, and Classes in Personal Religion. It is greatly hoped that this little book may prove of use in many ways, but especially in encouraging a revival of the beneficent but largely discarded custom of Family Prayers in the homes of our people.

WILLIAM SCARLETT
—from the 1972 Introduction

Preface

Among the rich privileges of my life, none is greater than standing, as Bishop of Missouri, in succession to Will Scarlett.

Dean of Christ Church Cathedral, St. Louis, and afterward Bishop, Will Scarlett tended this part of God's vineyard from 1922 to 1952. During that time he planted in the Missouri soil seeds of such potency that the fruits are still available to those who seek the nourishment necessary to follow after him in the ministry of Christ. They are the fruits that nourish Christian social conscience and fortify the desire to reach across parochial boundaries to engage in ecumenical and inter-faith life. It is the food which sustains a passion for creation and the awe and wonder which lie at the heart of his prayers.

In Will Scarlett true piety and a thirst for a just and equitable society were wonderfully met. The prayers contained in this little collection, splendidly restored to the church by Almus Thorp's initiative and his deft and gentle editorial hand, reveal someone who loved the church and knew that God had sent the Son to redeem the world. May they be prayers to make serene hearts and strong wills in another generation of those who seek to follow the One to whom Will Scarlett gave both heart and will.

Hays H. Rockwell
Ninth Bishop of Missouri
St. Louis
Pentecost, 1994

To Will One Thing

Father in Heaven! What is a man without Thee! What is all that he knows, vast accumulation though it be, but a chipped fragment if he does not know Thee! What is all his striving, could it even encompass a world, but a half-finished work if he does not know Thee: Thee the One, Who art one thing and Who art all! So may Thou give to the intellect wisdom to comprehend that one thing; to the heart, sincerity to receive this understanding; to the will, purity that wills only one thing.

—Søren Kierkegaard

O God of grace and truth, whom the heavens cannot contain, but who loves to dwell with those who are of contrite heart, look mercifully upon us as we seek your face. You are eternal and we are frail children of the dust; you are Holy and we are enmeshed in the passions and impulses of this flesh; your heart is Love and we seek our own. Yet, mean though we are, we are not wholly so. We are sick of our obsession with self. Help us to escape the tyranny of self by finding our brothers and sisters and living in them, by finding you and losing ourselves.

Give us grace to overcome the world's injustice, to hear the cries of the oppressed, to succor the fallen and to heal the victims of our inhumanity. Through Jesus Christ our Lord. Amen.

—Reinhold Niebuhr

O God, in the stillness of worship may we grow more sure of you. You are often closest to us when we feel you have forsaken us. The toil and thought of daily life leave us little time to think of you; but may the quiet of this prayer make us aware that though we forget you, you do not forget us. Perhaps we have grown careless, perhaps duty has lost its high solemnities, perhaps the altar fires have gone untended, perhaps your light within has been distrusted or ignored. As we withdraw awhile from all without, may we find you anew within, until all thought grows reverent again, all work is hallowed, and faith reconsecrates all common things as sacraments of love.

If your purposes have crossed our own and your will has defeated ours, enable us to trust the wisdom of your perfect love, and find your will to be our peace. If our wills have thwarted yours, give us clearer vision that we may see the better way before us and make your purposes our own.

So lead us back to meet you where we may have missed you before. Amen.

—W. E. Orchard

✠ ✠ ✠

O God, grant that we may desire you, and desiring you seek you, and seeking you find you, and finding you be satisfied in you forever. Amen.

—St. Francis Xavier

✠ ✠ ✠

O Lord, our only Saviour, so dwell within us that we may go forth with the light of hope in our eyes and the fire of inspiration on our lips, thy word on our tongues and your love in our hearts. Amen.

—Prayers for the City of God

Grant, O Lord God:

That we may wait, as servants standing in the presence of their Lord, for the slightest sign or hint of your will;

That we may welcome all truth, under whatever outward forms it is uttered;

That we may have grace to receive new thought gracefully, courteously, fairly, charitably, reverently;

That we may believe firmly that, however strange or startling, it may come from you whose ways are not as our ways or thoughts as our thoughts;

That we may bless every good deed, by whomsoever it is done;

That we may rise above all party cries and fashions to the vision of your eternal truth and goodness. Amen.

—Charles Kingsley

O God, without whose beauty and goodness our souls are unfed, without whose truthfulness our reason withers: Consecrate our lives to your will, giving us such purity of heart, such depth of faith, such steadfastness of purpose, that, in your good time, we may come to think your own thought after you; through Jesus Christ our Saviour. Amen.

—Henry S. Nash

Our God, in whom is our trust: strengthen us to regard not over much who is for us or who against us, but to see well to it that we be with you in everything we do. Amen.

—Thomas à Kempis

Deepen and quicken in us, O God, the sense of your presence. Make us to know and feel that you are more ready to teach than we to learn. Grant us dignity in our own eyes by taking us into your service. Humble us by laying bare before our eyes our littleness and our sin, and then exalt us by revealing yourself as our Counsellor, our Father, and our Friend; through Jesus Christ our Lord. Amen.

—Henry S. Nash

O God, Who are the light of the minds that know you, the life of the souls that love you, and the strength of the wills that serve you: Help us so to know you that we may truly love you, so to love you that we may fully serve you, whom to serve is perfect freedom; through Jesus Christ our Lord. Amen.

—Gelasian BCR

O God, the true sun of the world, ever rising and never going down; by your most wholesome appearing and sight you nourish and gladden all things in heaven and earth. Mercifully shine in our hearts that the night of darkness and sin being driven away by your brightness shining within our hearts, we may walk without stumbling, as in the daytime, and, being pure and clean from the works of darkness, may abound in all good works which you have prepared for us to walk in. Amen.

—Erasmus

O God, guide us, teach us, strengthen us, till we become such men and women as you would have us be; truthful and high-minded, brave and able, courteous, generous and useful;

Take from us, O God, all pride and vanity, boasting and forwardness, and give us the courage that shows itself by gentleness, the wisdom that shows itself by simplicity, and the power that shows itself by modesty. Amen.

—Charles Kingsley

O God, set our hearts at liberty from the service of ourselves, and let it be our meat and drink to do your will; through Jesus Christ our Lord. Amen.

—Henry S. Nash

O God, ever present with us, to whose wisdom our problems must seem so simple and easy: help us to stay our minds on Thee, that we may think clearly, see straight, and act according to your will, through Jesus Christ, our Master. Amen.

—Maude Royden

✤ ✤ ✤

Give me, O Lord, a steadfast heart, which no unworthy thought can drag down, an unconquered heart, which no tribulation can wear out; an upright heart, which no unworthy purpose can tempt aside. Bestow upon me understanding to know you, diligence to seek you, wisdom to find you and faithfulness that finally may embrace you. Amen.

—Thomas Aquinas

O God, in whom is no darkness at all, nor shadow cast by turning, forgive our feverish ways—our anxieties, our fears, our uncertainties. We are like children walking willfully and blindly in darkness while the world without is ablaze with light.

Open our eyes that we may see you, and our minds that we may understand and know you. Help us to make the great adventure of faith and discover the secret of peace, in finding you, the great Companion of our souls. Amen.

—William Scarlett

✛ ✛ ✛

Give to us, O Lord, a right discernment between that which comes first in our faith and that which follows after and when we would make much of that which cannot matter to Thee, recall us to the heart of our Christian profession; through Jesus Christ our Lord. Amen.

—Willard L. Sperry

✛ ✛ ✛

O God, give wings to our hopes, and rest to our fears. Give us courage; that believing in you we may dare high things for you. Save us from the little faith which makes us the victims of anxieties and fears, and puts us to shame and confusion. Give us dignity and worth by sending us some work to do for you; fire our wills to accomplish something for your Kingdom before we leave this world. May the Spirit that was in Jesus so possess our minds and wills that we may share His indignations, His purpose, and His radiant faith in Thee. Amen.

—William Scarlett

O God, let peace abound in our company. Purge out of every heart the lurking grudge. Give us grace and strength to forbear and persevere. Offenders ourselves, give us grace to accept and forgive offenders. Forgetful, help us to bear cheerfully the forgetfulness of others. Give us courage and gaiety and the quiet mind. Amen.

—Robert Louis Stevenson

O God and Father of us all, breathe upon us now your hallowed calm; lift the burden from our hearts, soothe the anxieties of our minds, and send peace into our souls.

Forgive the disorder, the fever, the vain purpose of our lives. We have made haste as those who believe not. We have been desperate as those who lead a forlorn hope; we have not trusted in you. We have spent our days contrary to your plainest laws. Our eyes have been fixed to earth, and rarely lifted to the hills. We have not silenced ourselves to hear, nor been patient to understand. We have been fretful as children, comfortless as those who never knew you. We have spent our strength on things that do not profit, and laboured for the bread that perishes while your free and glorious gifts have lain near to us unappropriated and often spurned.

Help us now to stand awhile in the shelter of your shadowing wings, and to be still; to look out again upon life with new vision, that we may understand; to wait for the revelation of your will that shall make us calm and strong. Amen.

—W. E. Orchard

O God, give me strength to live another day. Let me not turn coward before its difficulties or prove recreant to its duties. Let me not lose faith in my fellow-men. Keep me sweet and sound of heart, in spite of ingratitude, treachery, meanness. Preserve me from minding little stings or giving them. Help me to keep my heart clean, and to live so honestly and fearlessly that no outward failure can dishearten me or take away the joy of conscious integrity. Open wide the eyes of my soul that I may see good in all things. Grant me this day some new vision of your truth, inspire me with the spirit of joy and gladness and make me the cup of strength to suffering souls. Amen.

—Phillips Brooks

Heavenly Father, for all Thy goodness to us, we bless and praise Thy Holy Name:

For the beauty of this good earth, for the liveliness of flowers and changing seasons, for trees in winter darkly etched against a steel-gray sky, for racing clouds and starry nights:

For our friends and all the friendliness which has blessed our lives:

For human love which admits us so intimately into Thy Divine Presence:

For life itself with all its glory, its challenge, its opportunity:

Keep us close to Thee, we pray Thee, that none of life be wasted, and make us channels and agents of Thy good will in a troubled world. Amen.

—William Scarlett

O God, from whose gift come sunshine and friendship and the glory of a summer's day, who in the common things of daily life gives to us your very self; strengthen and refresh us that we may seek you eagerly, find you surely, and serve you faithfully; through Jesus Christ our Lord. Amen.

✣ ✣ ✣

Grant us, O God, that inner peace and strength and courage, that royalty of inner happiness, which come of living close to Thee. Amen.

—William Scarlett

✣ ✣ ✣

O Master of Life, without whose aid we are as dust that builds on dust: Be now and ever our Great Companion. For the sake of those we love, free us from vanity. For the sake of our nation and our race, cleanse us of our fears. For the lifting up of the fallen, the comforting of the lonely, make us gentle and make us strong. We ask it for Christ's sake. Amen.

—Henry S. Nash

✣ ✣ ✣

Almighty God, our heavenly Father, from whom comes every good and perfect gift, we call to remembrance your loving kindness and your tender mercies which have been ever of old, and with grateful hearts we lift up to you the voice of our thanksgiving.

For the life you have given us, and the world in which we live;

For the work we are enabled to do, and the truth we are permitted to learn; for whatever good there has been in our past lives, and for all the hopes and aspirations which lead us on toward better things;

For all the gladness of life; for our homes and our home-blessings; for the love, sympathy, and good will of our friends: we praise you, O God.

For the gift of your Son Jesus Christ, and all the hopes which are ours as His disciples; for the presence and inspiration of your Holy Spirit, and for all the ministers of your truth and grace;

For communion with you, the Father of our spirits; for the light and peace which are gained through trust and obedience, and the darkness and disquietude which befall us when we disobey your laws and follow our lower desires and selfish passions;

For all the discipline of life; for the tasks and trials by which we are trained to patience, self-knowledge and self-conquest, and brought into closer sympathy with our suffering brethren; for troubles which have lifted us nearer to you and drawn us into deeper fellowship with Jesus Christ;

For the sacred and tender ties which bind us to the unseen world; for the faith which dispels the shadows of earth, and fills the last moments of life with the light of an immortal hope: we praise you, O God.

O God of all grace and love, we have praised you with our lips; grant that we may also praise you in consecrated and faithful lives; through Jesus Christ our Lord. Amen.

O Lord, we pray thee look in thine infinite pity upon this, thy world; for lo! day is at hand, and thy children must soon awake to life, and toil, and temptation. Let thy Holy Spirit wait to meet with each one of us upon the threshold of the dawn, and lead us through this coming day. Like as a father pitieth his children so dost thou pity all the woeful and heavy-hearted. Look upon all those who must awake to their griefs, speak comfortably to them; remember those in pain who must take up heavy burdens! Look upon the hungry, the rich, the evil, and the good, that in this new day, finding something of thy mercy, each may give thanks unto thee, for thy goodness and mercy endureth forever. Amen.

—Jeffery Farnol

✤   ✤   ✤

Our God, who art the Father of our spirits, when evening falls and strange feelings, ancient fears, obstinate questionings, rise within us, we turn to thee, who alone holdest the secret of thine own creation.

We believe that some kindly purpose lies beyond our coming into this world: not chance, nor fate, nor punishment can explain life; but only love. We feel sure of this because of thy word in our hearts, and because of thy word made flesh.

We have stood before a lonely cross whereon One died, despised and rejected of men, and there we have learned how pain and death need bring no defeat to thy purposes, and hold no contradiction of thy love.

Thou hast placed within our trembling hands the strands of life whose issues are in eternity. How shall we live aright; we are sinful, weak, wilful? Be very merciful to thy children, Father. The lessons of life are difficult unless One interpret to us. Give us tonight thine interpretation of all that we are, and are destined yet to be. So shall we realize thy salvation and be glad in thee all our days. Amen.

—W. E. Orchard

Abide with us, O Lord, this night, that the brightness of thy love may be around us and the darkness be not dark. Abide with us, O Lord, this night, for in loneliness we are not alone if thou be nigh. Abide with the sick, the sorrowful, the forsaken, and the weary, to strengthen, to comfort, to cheer, and to give rest. Shield us all from that darkness of the soul which seeth thee not, that loneliness of the heart which heareth not thy voice. Abide with us through life, and in the valley of the shadow of death forsake us not, but bid us be of good courage, for thou art with us still. Amen.

A Declaration of Faith

We believe in Jesus Christ, and in the beauty of the gospel that began in Bethlehem.
We believe in him whose spirit glorified a little town;
>   Of whose coming only shepherds saw the sign,
>   And for whom the crowded inn could find no room.
We believe in him whom the kings of the earth ignored
>   And the proud could never understand;
>   Whose paths were among the common people,
>   Whose welcome came from men of hungry hearts.
We believe in him who proclaimed the love of God to be invincible:
>   Whose cradle was a mother's arms,
>   Whose home in Nazareth had love for its only wealth,
>   Who looked at men and made them see what his love saw in them;
>   Who by his love brought sinners back to purity,
>   And lifted human weakness up to meet the strength of God.
We confess our everlasting need of God:

The need of forgiveness for our greed and selfishness
The need of life for empty souls,
The need of love for hearts grown cold.
We acknowledge the glory of all that is like Christ:
The steadfastness of friends,
the blessedness of homes,
The beauty of compassion,
The miracle of many hearts made kind at Christmas,
The courage of those who dare to resist all passion, hate, and violence.
We believe that only by love expressed shall the earth at length be purified.
And we acknowledge in Christ
A faith that sees beyond the partial fact,
A trust in life redeemed that looks beyond our present evil;
And we pray that this redemption may begin in us who kneel and say together now—(The Lord's Prayer)

—W. Russell Bowie

Our Father, who has been likened unto a potter working at the wheel, taking the unformed clay and molding it into a pleasing likeness: who, if a flaw is revealed in the vessel does not cast it aside as useless but puts it again on the wheel, patiently shaping it toward greater beauty:

So take and use us, thy faltering children. Bring us again under the discipline of thy love and justice; confirm and fulfill thine intent for us, mold us into the likeness of the men and women thou would have us be:

And grant us continual growth in knowledge and love of thee and in courageous dedication to thy will; through him who is, the Saviour of this imperilled world. Amen.

—William Scarlett

Earth Shall Be Fair

O Master of the hearts of men, make us ill content with any peace save that of our Saviour, who won his peace after he had made the world's ills his own. Amen.

—Henry S. Nash

O God, whose property is always to have mercy: Help us to live so close to thee that we may acquire the pity which takes us out of ourselves and puts us in others' places, which makes us sit where they sit, see through their eyes, feel their neglects, frustrations and injustices as our own; the pity which resents and redresses the wrongs of others as readily as our own; the pity which is the Spirit of a just and loving God moving in our hearts. Keep our compassion wise and fair, sensitive, courageous and strong to heal the victims of our inhumanity. We pray in the name of Jesus Christ, our Lord. Amen.

—William Scarlett

O God, we lay hold of thy Cross, as of a staff that can stand unshaken when the floods run high. The tale told us is no story of some far-away land: it is this world, and not another—this world with all its miseries and its slaughter and its ruin—that thou hast entered to redeem, by thine agony and bloody sweat. Amen.

—H. Scott Holland

O Lord Jesus Christ, who art not ashamed to own as thy brethren the meanest of humankind, and

Who hast said,

"Inasmuch as ye did it unto one of the least of these my brethren, ye did it unto me;"

Make us so to identify with all humanity, that we may labour for the things that belong unto our peace.

O Lord Jesus, who didst not refuse to drink the cup which the Father had given thee, saying, "Not my will, but thine be done;"

Cleanse us from all sin, that we may have fellowship one with another, and serve the Living God, in thee and through thee, who came not to be ministered unto, but to minister, and to give thy life a ransom for many. Amen.

—Prayers for the City of God

Our Father, though the heavens can not contain thee, thou dost dwell with those who are of a contrite heart. In thy sight the proud are abased and those who humble themselves are exalted. In thy presence all our deceits and disguises are without avail, for thou settest our secret sins in the light of thy countenance and we become conscious of all our vanities and cheap ambitions. Save us from pride and arrogance so that in thy presence the vision of what we might be will convict us of what we are.

When we penetrate the central mysteries of life in thy presence contrition and gratitude mingle in our hearts, for we see the evils of life which we create and suffer to exist, but we also realize the beauty of the world which thou hast made. We thank thee for everything about us which ministers to our better nature: for the greatness and glory of the world, for the majesty and serenity of nature and for the infinities which carry our imagination beyond the limits of our comprehension. We thank thee for the history of our race with its glimpses of nobility amidst human sin, and for every assurance that though we are mean and petty we are not wholly so. We praise thee for the beauty wrought by craftsmen and artists and for all symbols of perfection which disturb our ease and incite our ambition. We are grateful for the songs of faith sung by thy children in every age and for the heritage of faith bequeathed to us, so that when we are perplexed, we are not perplexed unto despair. We thank thee for the pressure of duty and for the discipline of responsibilities. Above all we thank thee for the Lord of life whose tragic majesty wins ever and again from our hearts an ennobling affection and who, being lifted up, lifts all folk unto him.

Have mercy upon us for appropriating so rich a life with so little concern for those to whom beauty and joy are denied, whether by the cruelties of nature, the inhumanities of men or by their own limitations. Since we are debtors both to the wise and the unwise, teach us to discharge our debts to those who have given us much by serving those who need us greatly.

Teach us to know that the perils and pains through which our generation is passing are the just deserts for our sins and those of our fathers. Reveal thyself to us in our daily life that we may know thee as the prophets have known thee—a God of both wrath and mercy. So may we be moved to contrition by thy wrath upon our sins and to gratitude by thy sustaining mercy.

In all things subject us to the spirit and the mind of Christ in whose name we pray. Amen.

—Reinhold Niebuhr

O God, if of all thy good gifts we may have but one, let that be the Spirit of Christ;

> Crown the Church of Christ with the Spirit of Christ;
> Fill our lives to overflowing with the Spirit of Christ;
> May the spirit which was in Christ so possess our minds and wills that we may share his purpose, his indignations, his faith in thee and his faith in us.

> May the Spirit of Christ shame our indifference, shatter our complacency, move us to deep concern for all mankind, and set us on fire to bring this world under thy Reign. Amen.

—William Scarlett

✛ ✛ ✛

Grant to us, O God, more and more of the Spirit of Christ; the Spirit that suffereth long and is kind; the Spirit that is magnanimous, generous, lofty of purpose; the Spirit that is not stirred to envy, nor moved by self-importance, and which does not jealously seek and insist on its right; the Spirit which hides the faults of others and endeavors to believe the best about all people; the Spirit that beareth all things, believeth all things, endureth all things and which never fails.

> Let us never be overcome by evil, but endeavor to overcome evil with good.

> Enable us to love our enemies, to bless those who curse us, to do good to those who hate us,

> That we may be inclusive in our good will as is our Father in Heaven who maketh his sun to shine on the evil and on the good and sendeth his rain on the just and on the unjust.

> We pray in the name of Christ, our Lord. Amen.

O God, author of the world's joy, bearer of the world's pain, make us glad that we are thy children and have inherited the world's burden; deliver us from the luxury of cheap melancholy; and, at the heart of all our trouble and sorrow, let unconquerable gladness dwell; through our Lord and Saviour Jesus Christ. Amen.

—Henry S. Nash

O God, forgive the poverty, the pettiness, the childish folly of our prayers. Listen not to our words, but to the desires that cannot be uttered; hearken not to our petitions, but to the crying of our need. So often we pray for that which is already ours, neglected and unappropriated; so often for that which never can be ours; so often for that which we must win ourselves; and then labor endlessly for that which can only come to us in prayer.

How often we have prayed for the coming of thy Kingdom, and yet we have barred the way. We have no trust in our own strength or loyalty or courage.

Give us to love thy will, and to seek thy Kingdom first of all. Sweep away our fears, our compromises, our weakness, lest at last we be found fighting against thee. Amen.

—W. E. Orchard

Lord, make us instruments of your peace: Where there is hatred, let us sow love; where there is injury, pardon; where there is discord, union; where there is doubt, faith; where there is despair, hope; where there is darkness, light; where there is sadness, joy, for your mercy and for your truth's sake. Amen.

—St. Francis of Assisi

Almighty God, who keeps ever bright before our eyes the vision of a better world: forbid us contentment of soul in neglect of the misery of so many of your children, and help us not to shirk our part in the prophet's task; through Jesus Christ our Lord. Amen.

—Willard L. Sperry

Most Holy and Most Merciful Father, give us the wisdom born of love to see beneath the surface of the human lives we touch and to understand the hidden streams and motives moving there—the hopes and fears, the failures and successes, the aspirations and struggles which are a part of every life. Give us the discernment to sense the factors unknown to others—the burden that is borne silently, the closed doors, the handicaps of life, the hidden heroisms, the hidden tragedies, the treacheries and betrayals, the evil heritage which must be carried as an undeserved legacy of the past. May we look out upon all people with the eyes of the heart as well as with the eyes of the head; and make us endlessly, incredibly merciful. Amen.

—William Scarlett

Almighty Father, who settest our minds on fire with the vision of a more perfect society here on earth, in which justice, righteousness and peace shall be established, according to thy will; grant to us the inspiration of thy Presence, that we may think always those things that are just, and do those things which are right; that so thy will may be done on earth as it is in Heaven: through Christ, our Lord. Amen.

—William Scarlett

Almighty God, our Heavenly Father, who lovest all and forgettest none, we bring to thee our supplications for all thy children: For all whom we love and for whom we watch and care:

For all who have blessed us with kindness, led us with patience, restored us with sympathy and whose love has covered a multitude of our sins:

For all who have wished or done us ill, that thou wouldst turn their hearts to penitence and ours to pity and blessing:

For all prisoners refugees and captives; for all women and children suffering from oppression, that thou wilt manifest thy mercy towards them, and make the heart of man merciful as thine own:

For all on whom thou hast laid the cross of suffering, the sick in body or in mind:

For all who are troubled by the suffering or sin of those they love:

For all who are visited by worldly loss, that in dark times they may find the peace of God:

For all who are absorbed in their own grief, that they may be raised to share the sorrows of others, and know the secret and blessed fellowship of the Cross:

For all who are suffering because of their faithfulness to conviction and duty, that renunciation may bring strength, and sacrifice, joy; and that they may come at last to an open reward:

For all perplexed and over-shadowed with doubt, that light may arise in their darkness:

For all who are tried by passionate temptations, or mean suggestions, that thy mercy may be their salvation:

For all who are lonely in the midst of others' joy, that they may know thee as their Friend and Comforter:

For the infirm and aged and for all who are passing through the valley of death, that they may find comfort and strength in God, and light at even time:

For all forgotten by us, but dear to thee:

O God our Father, have regard to our intercessions, answer them according to thy will, and make us the channels of thine infinite pity and helpfulness; through Jesus Christ, our Lord. Amen.

✠ ✠ ✠

O God, keep us from narrowing and limiting our affections. Open our hearts to the forgotten peoples of our world. When the comforts and joys of friendship and family life sustain us, let the thought of the places where our brethren must live, the house of shame, the prisons, the refugee camps, the city streets not fail to visit us. May we count all joy unworthy if it has not in it the pain of sorrow over these for whom we pray. Amen.

—Henry S. Nash

✠ ✠ ✠

O God, we dedicate ourselves anew to thee and to thy service. Pour into our hearts such love for thee that we may indeed love our neighbors as ourselves—a love that leaps the boundaries of race or color or creed or kind, that knows no distinction of class, that reaches out a saving hand even unto the least of these our brethren. Fill our lives with the single motive of service, and use us, Lord, use us for thine own purposes, just as thou wilt, and when, and where: through Christ, our Master. Amen.

—William Scarlett

Almighty Father, Maker of the stars, Master of the nations of earth, we ask thy favor on our country;

That we may never grow weary of our task nor doubt the final triumph of our aims, grant to us unconquerable faith, infinite patience and confidence that truth if made known will win its way.

Grant us flexibility of mind that we may create the conditions which make all peoples free and equal, enhance human dignity and self-respect and establish economic security for all;

Bind upon each of us a stern sense of our accountability to thee, that we may devise those things which are just, rise above every group or sectional prejudice and make the good of all our aim. So may we take our place among those who labor that government of the people, by the people, for the people may not perish from the earth. Amen.

—William Scarlett

Merciful Father, we pray for all that sit in darkness and in the shadow of death, that the Dayspring from on high may visit them; for the poor and oppressed, for those that dwell amid ugliness and squalor; for those who toil beyond their strength, for those without pleasure in the work of their hands, and without hope of rest; and for all who are trampled under foot by men. Raise up deliverance for the peoples. Amen.

O Christ, Word of God made flesh to dwell among us, whom we adore as our Lord and Saviour:

Grant to us the courage to follow the promptings of thy Spirit wherever they may lead us;

Give us reverence for thy words of Eternal Truth, but also recollection that the letter killeth and it is the Spirit which giveth life;

Give us the wisdom, in these days when no decision is simple, to sense the direction in which the Kingdom of God lies, and the will to take that path;

Give us the love which would heal offenders, but would make no peace with oppression and injustice; give us the mercy which tempers justice without losing sight of Justice;

Give us the tolerance to understand and bear with others, but also the discernment to know where tolerance ends and lines must be drawn;

Mould us nearer to thy pattern; help us to lose ourselves in thy service, to reverence all persons as objects of God's concern, to fight for social justice and to establish the conditions which make for human dignity, freedom and peace. Amen.

—William Scarlett

O God, who hast sent us to school in this strange life of ours, and hast set us tasks which test all our courage, trust, and fidelity; may we not spend our days complaining or fretting but give ourselves to learn of life and to profit by every experience. Make us strong to endure.

Grant by thy grace that we may not be found wanting in the hour of crisis. When the battle is set, may we know on which side we ought to be, and when the day goes hard, may our place be found where the fight is fiercest. If we faint, may we not be faithless; if we fall, may it be while facing the foe. Amen.

—W. E. Orchard

A Benediction

Unto God's gracious mercy and protection we commit this great city; all who abide in this place; all who here bear the authority of government and administration: the Lord bless and keep us all, especially the impoverished, the neglected, the sufferers and the unemployed;

The Lord increase in us all a sense of community;

The Lord strengthen in us the certainty that we are members one of another, and that if one member suffers all the members suffer with it;

The Lord quicken into action the conviction that we are all of us responsible for all of us, that we may build a nobler city, in equality, in justice, in fraternity;

And may the peace and strength and beauty of God abide in our hearts, to steady our minds and quicken our wills to do his will, now and ever. Amen.

—William Scarlett

All Her People One

O God, from the murmur and subtlety of suspicion with which we vex one another, give us rest. Make a new beginning, and mingle again the kindred of the nations in the alchemy of love, and with some finer essence of forbearance and forgiveness temper our minds. Amen.

—Aristophanes

Eternal Father, in whom the whole family of the earth is one, over-riding our minor distinctions of race and nationality and economic class: breathe thy spirit into our hearts, into the hearts of all people of good will in every land, that we and they may establish a new order wherein we all may live together in trust and fellowship, in justice and peace.

Illumine the darkness of our minds that in thy light we may see light and think thine own thoughts after thee and serve the greater glory of God by advancing the greater good of all people; through Jesus Christ our Lord. Amen.

—William Scarlett

Eternal Father who showest thy people the way on which they should go: Turn our feet from the paths of destruction and towards the City of God, that we may fashion on this earth that new world for which thy Son was content long since to die. Amen.

Almighty God, Maker of the Stars, Master of Life, whose Holy Spirit of Truth is sweeping through our world like a mighty wind, overturning old institutions, forcing us to re-examine old traditions and loyalties, unsettling all our solutions until they are settled aright: Grant to us in these days a clearer vision of thy Being and Beauty, thy Holiness, thy Justice, thy Pity, thy Concern for all, that touched by thy Love we may give ourselves to thy service.

Grant us grace to overcome the world's injustice, to hear the cries of the oppressed, to succor the needy and to heal the victims of man's long inhumanity to man:

Give us a moving conviction of the unity of all humankind in thee, that we may organize our world accordingly. Give us a profound sense of human solidarity, that we may feel injustice anywhere as a blow at ourselves, and resent and redress the wrongs of others as readily as our own.

We do not ask that thou wilt keep us safe, but that we may be loyal to high ends at whatever cost. Give us the courage resolutely to stand for the hard right, gladly to suffer hardship for the sake of a better world, fearlessly to strike a blow for human freedom and social justice.

Give us the inner strength and peace which come of living close to thee, seeking to know and to do thy will; and use us, Lord, use us for thine own purposes, just as thou wilt and when and where.

Once more we make the spirit of the Master's prayer our own: Our Father, thy Kingdom come, thy will be done on earth . . . Amen.

—William Scarlett

Our Father, who hast borne with us far beyond all human merit, move our hearts to penitence:

We have known thy moral law through the prophets of mankind; we have caught in Jesus Christ a vision of thy being and beauty and thy concern for our world; we have prayed for centuries that thy kingdom might come and thy will be done on earth;

But we have acted as though the things we touch and weigh and measure alone were the real things, and we have treated thy moral law and thy sovereignty over us as negligible.

We turn to thee, our Father, asking that thou wilt have mercy upon us and renew a right spirit within us.

As thy Spirit moved on the face of the waters to bring order out of chaos, do thou move in our hearts that our faith in thee may be rekindled and our minds glow again with the conviction of thy presence;

As we draw closer to thee may we be knit together in one fellowship transcending all our divisions, that we may build a new world in which all peoples may live their lives in the full dignity of thy children. Amen.

—William Scarlett

Fix thou our steps, O Lord, that we stagger not at the uneven motions of the world, but go steadily on our way, neither censuring our journey by the weather we meet, nor turning aside for anything that befalls us. Amen.

—John Weston

Let us pray together in silence:

Let us pray first for our own families, for father, for mother, whom we yet have, or whom perhaps we have lost awhile; for husband or wife; for children, or brother, or sister, or loved ones. (Silence)

Let us extend our prayer for the Family to include our Nation, and every group within the same, that we may come together in faith and fellowship and build a nobler land in justice, in fraternity, in peace. (Silence)

Let us now extend our prayer for the Family to the uttermost bounds of the earth; let us pray for every Nation, every Race, every Creed; realizing that under God we are all one Family, members one of another, responsible one for the other; that as our physical world has become one, so also we may realize our common humanity and our common destiny. (Silence)

—William Scarlett

✛ ✛ ✛

O God Most High, who rulest in the kingdom of men, and givest it to whomever thou wilt, cast out from us, we pray thee, the spirit of domination:

Give us the enthusiasm of service, that we may not claim universal supremacy for our own customs, opinions, and forms of government, that we may not regard each variation from our own standards of thought as the result of ignorance and degeneracy, that we may not press patriotism into arrogant self-assertion.

Keep us from the spirit of worldliness, lest we make our power the counsellor of our designs or our material interests the standard of our success;

Give us gratitude for the variety of thy gifts, that we may not be dwarfed and chilled by the narrowing of our sympathies;

And grant that we may commend to others the blessings we have received, that we may protect, foster and develop human forces which have not yet reached their full growth, that by spiritual quickening we may help to mould a new world to greater freedom. Amen.

—Bishop Westcott

Behold, O God, our striving after a truer and more abiding order. Give us visions which bring back a lost glory to the earth, and dreams which foreshadow the better order you have prepared for us. Scatter every excuse of frailty and unworthiness. Open to us a clearer prospect of our work. Give us strength according to our day gladly to welcome and gratefully to fulfill it. Amen.

—Bishop Westcott

Enlighten our minds, O God, to discern your eternal laws standing steadfast and unchanged amidst the storms of human passion and the strife of human wills.

Burn up the overgrowth of our luxury; melt away our class selfishness; fuse our cold prudence into clear-sighted and self-forgetful energy, and make our whole people glow with renewed faith and trust in you. Amen.

—F. P. Cobbe

God of all nations,
We pray for all the peoples of the earth:
For those who are consumed in mutual hatred and bitterness:
For those who make bloody war upon their neighbours:
For those who tyrannously oppress:
For those who groan under cruelty and subjection.

We pray for all those who bear rule and responsibility:
For the ignorant, the wretched, the enslaved.

We beseech you to teach us to live together in peace
No one exploiting the weak, no one hating the strong,
Each race working out its own destiny,
Unfettered, self-respecting, fearless.

Teach us to be worthy of freedom,
Free from social wrong, free from individual oppression
    and contempt,
Pure of heart and hand, despising none, defrauding none,
Giving to all—in all the dealings of life—
The honour we owe to those who are your children,
Whatever their colour, their race or language.

—J. S. Hayland

Voices are crying from the dust of Tyre,
From Karnak and the stones of Babylon,
"We raised our pillars upon self-desire
And perished in the large gaze of the sun."

We thank you, O God, for the freedom of worship, of thought, of speech, we have enjoyed. Let our religion not divide us from our fellow men, but knit us together as children of one God, in earnest and universal kindness, even to those who disown or scorn you. Amen.

—Francis Newman

Overrule, we pray you, O God, the passions and designs of men. Let your strong hand control the nations and bring forth out of the present discord a harmony more perfect than we can conceive, a new humility, a new understanding, a new purity and sincerity, a new sense of reality, a new hunger and thirst for your love to rule the earth. Amen.

Grant, O Lord, that we may approach every question of foreign policy from the point of view of our creed, that our noblest thoughts may be purified and strengthened; that we may check in ourselves and in others every temper which makes for violence, all ungenerous judgments, all presumptuous claims, all promptings of self-assertion, isolation, arrogance and passion; that we may endeavor to understand the needs, the feelings, the endowments, the traditional aspirations of other countries; that we may gladly, and patiently, do what lies in us to remove all suspicions and misunderstandings; thus may we honor all people. Amen.

—Bishop Westcott

O God, who hast made man in thine own likeness and who dost love all whom thou has made, suffer us not, because of difference in race, color or condition, to separate ourselves from others and thereby from thee; but teach us the unity of thy family and the universality of thy love. As thy Son, our Saviour, was born of a Hebrew mother and ministered first to his brethren of the House of Israel, but rejoiced in the faith of a Syro-Phoenician woman and of a Roman soldier, and suffered his cross to be carried by a man of Africa, teach us also, while loving and serving our own, to enter into the communion of the whole human family. And forbid that, from pride of birth and hardness of heart, we should despise any for whom Christ died or injure any in whom he lives. Amen.

—Mornay Williams

For all thy goodness to us, our Father, we bless and praise thy holy Name: make us, we pray thee, channels of thy will for a better world for all peoples; through Jesus Christ, our Lord. Amen.

—William Scarlett

O God our Father, in whom is calmness and peace: make up, we beseech thee, the dissensions which divide us from each other, and bring us back into that unity of love which is the likeness of thy nature, that bound together in thy Spirit, we may know that peace of thine which maketh all things one; through Jesus Christ our Lord. Amen.

O God, who has made of one blood all nations of men to dwell on the face of the whole earth, look down in mercy upon the nations of the world:

Drive away the evil passions of hatred, suspicion and fear which have encompassed us:

Grant that united in good understanding, we may establish a new order wherein the nations may live together in trust and fellowship, each in the praise of great achievements, and the rivalry of good and beneficent deeds, truthful, honest and just in our dealings one with another, and following in all things the way of our Lord and Savior, Jesus Christ. Amen.

—Bishop Gore

Almighty God, who sitteth above the circle of the earth and stretcheth out the heavens as a curtain, who bringeth princes to nothing, and maketh the judges of the earth as vanity: look in mercy on our world;

Grant to the leaders of this nation, adventurous and generous statemanship, that we may exercise our power and responsibility, not for ourselves alone, but for all people in all lands, that a brighter day may dawn on history;

Make us, people of these United States, strong to assist in the maintenance of justice and stability in the world, to feed the hungry and to lay strong and deep foundations for a more just and ordered life for all thy children, that thy will may be done on our earth. Amen.

—William Scarlett

Increase, O God, the spirit of neighborliness among us; that in peril we may uphold one another, in suffering tend one another, and in homelessness, loneliness or exile befriend one another. Grant us brave and enduring hearts that we may strengthen one another, till the disciplines and testing of these days be ended, and you again give peace in our time; through Jesus Christ our Lord. Amen.

—English Shelter Prayer

A Declaration of Belief

I believe in God, the creator of heaven and of earth, Lord of all power and might;

I believe in Jesus Christ, in whom the grace and glory of God became incarnate;

I believe in the Holy Spirit by whom the heavenly flame is brought to human souls;

I believe in the oneness of him who is made manifest in all things great and good.

I acknowledge the law of God which is written in the majesty of sun and stars;

I acknowledge the truth of God within which alone we can be free;

I acknowledge the love of God by which alone we are redeemed;

I acknowledge the fellowship of all saints
    Who learned of Christ and lived for him
    Who carried in their hearts the flame of consecration and courage,
    Who dared and endured and triumphed even in defeat:
    The evangelists, the apostles, and the martyrs,
    The singers of the triumph of the soul,

The lovers and the servants of humankind,
Who gave their lives, and in the giving found all life
fulfilled,
Who in their gentleness were great.
Through them and unto God I lift my soul in thankfulness
and in eternal praise. Amen.

—W. Russell Bowie

By What Shore

"Now I, for one, cannot believe that within a few years my attempt to understand the Universe will have ceased. So, as I come to the end of these lectures, I turn to whatever awaits me with hope and courage. The world is full of surprises and perplexities: but it is not a chaos. There is order within it. Reason and beauty and much goodness have gone into its making. I am, like each of yourselves, one of its children. Our high thoughts and hopes and desires belong to the life of the Spirit manifested within it. Behind the world, controlling Nature, is the Creative Spirit to Whom we are somehow akin. That Spirit is not a cold foe working through blind and pitiless forces; but is the source of our aspirations, friendly to our search for knowledge, the kindly guardian of our destinies. Therefore I am certain that our search will not end with death: labour and struggle will not be in vain. At the last we shall know even as we are known.

"To no companion of earth's short journey need we give an everlasting farewell. What we begin here we shall finish hereafter, if indeed it be worth the finishing. The fact that life is short and precarious matters little, inasmuch as those who have travelled with us here shall be our companions beyond the grave, if we and they alike seek the City of God."

—Ernest William Barnes

We seem to give *him* back to thee, dear God, who gavest *him* to us. Yet as thou didst not lose *him* in giving, so we have not lost *him* by *his* return. Not as the world giveth, givest thou, O Lover of Souls! What thou givest, thou takest not away. For what is thine is ours always, if we are thine. And life is eternal; and love is immortal; and death is only a horizon; and a horizon is nothing save the limit of our sight. Lift us up, strong Son of God, that we may see further; cleanse our eyes that we may see more clearly; draw us closer to thyself that we may know ourselves nearer to our beloved who are with thee. And while thou dost prepare a place for us, prepare us for the happy place, and that where they are, and thou art, we too may be. Amen.

Be thou with *him,* our Father, and lead *him* gently through the great transition from life through death to Life again—where *he* may meet thee face to face, know fully even as *he* has been fully known, go from strength to strength and mount up with wings as an eagle in the employment of *his* gifts in thy service. Amen.

—William Scarlett

O God of all the living, we thank thee for the happy memory of those whom thou hast called out of this transitory life into the eternal joy of thy presence. Thine they were upon the earth, as we are thine; and thine are they and we in differing experience still. Though our eyes cannot see them and our ears are deaf to their remembered voices, we bless thee that they are never absent from thy loving care. We thank thee for their lives of earthly service, for the happy days we spent in their companionship, the example of their faith and patience, the teaching of their words and deeds, and for their share in heaven's new opportunities of service. We confess to thee our neglects and transgressions, our coldness and misapprehension while they lived upon the earth, which we may no more confess to them. Our hearts have rest, knowing that thy love changeth not and that they see thy face with unobstructed vision. Help us so to live that they may welcome us with joy when thou shalt call us to thyself at last; through Jesus Christ our Lord. Amen.

—W. E. Gladstone

O God, who art, and wast, and art to come, before whose face the generations rise and pass away: age after age the living seek thee, and find that of thy faithfulness there is no end. Our fathers in their pilgrimage walked by thy guidance, and rested on thy compassion: still to their children be thou the cloud by day, the fire by night. Where but in thee have we a covert from the storm or shadow from the heat of life? In our manifold temptations, thou alone knowest and art ever nigh: in our prosperity and ease, it is thy Spirit only that can wean us from our pride, and keep us low. O thou sole source of peace and righteousness, take now the veil from every heart, and join us in one communion with thy prophets and saints who have trusted in thee, and were not ashamed. Not of our worthiness, but of thy tender mercy, hear our prayer. Amen.

—James Martineau

O God, the source of all that is good and beautiful and true, whose Spirit nourishes the souls of those who stay their minds on thee, we praise thee for thy goodness revealed in the lives of those who in their generations have been lights of the world; for their wisdom, tolerance, understanding and love freely given us. We thank thee for their vision of a more just and equal world, their steadfast striving to achieve their goal, their courage under adversity, their selfless service of the common good. May we take fire from their example and become like them true servants of God and of each other. Amen.

—William Scarlett

O God, who art Truth, O God, who art Spirit, help us in spirit and in truth to worship thy great name; not acknowledging thee in one place or at one time only but in every place, and at every time, in all we do and all we see, in our work and in our rest, in our laughter and our tears, in loneliness and in friendship, in the eye of day and in the shadow of night, beneath the open sky as in the house of prayer, in the fullness of health and strength as in the valley of the shadow of death, through which O Heavenly Father, do thou in thy mercy bear us to life and light and love. Amen.

Father of lights, by whose hand the fires of the sun are fed, and who hast kindled in our hearts the desire to know: We bless thee for leading us into a life wherein light and darkness are wondrously mingled. For the darkness and for the light we praise thee. O thou in whose being the simplicity and mystery of life do meet together, cleanse our prayers with the sanctity of reason, ennoble our reasonings with the majesty of prayer, and so bring us onward through darkness and through light, till we behold the Power that maketh the stars and the Love that exalteth our hearts, through him who is the Light of the world, our Saviour Jesus Christ. Amen.

—Henry S. Nash

✤ ✤ ✤

O Lord, by all your dealings with us, whether of joy or pain, of light or darkness, let us be brought to you. Let us value no treatment of thy grace simply because it makes us happy or because it makes us sad, because it gives us or denies us what we want; but may all that you send us bring us to you, that knowing your perfectness we may be sure that in every disappointment you are still loving us, and in every darkness you are still enlightening us, and in every enforced idleness you are still using us; yea, in every death you are giving us life, as in his death you gave life to your Son our Saviour Jesus Christ. Amen.

—Phillips Brooks

✤ ✤ ✤

Teach us, good Lord, to serve thee as thou deservest, to give and not to count the cost, to fight and not to heed the wounds, to toil and not to seek for rest, to labor and not to ask for any reward save that of knowing that we do thy will. Amen.

—Loyola

Litanies

Most holy and merciful God, the strength of the weak, the rest of the weary, and the refuge of your children in every time of need; hear us while we pray:

When our hearts are growing cold and dead, and we are losing our vision of your face, and living as though life had no spiritual reality:

help us, O God;

When the evil memories of the past trouble us, and we mourn over early hopes and dreams unrealized, over light within us turned to darkness and strength to weakness:

help us, O God;

When we are tempted to mean and wicked ways, and sin puts on the garments which make it seem less sinful in our sight:

help us, O God;

When we are called to difficult duty, to work in loneliness, and to bear burdens hard to be borne; when we are weary of our work and think it fruitless, and duty is painful because it seems unprofitable:

help us, O God;

When the unknown future troubles us, and amid our fears and anxieties we forget your eternal love and care:

help us, O God;

Stir up our wills to seek you and to find you, that you being our companion and guide we may faithfully follow after Christ, our Master. Amen.

An Act of Praise

Let us praise God:

> For the day, for the glory and warmth of the sun, for the stir of life, and for honest toil that wins food and rest.

> *God be praised for the day.*

For the earth, the sustainer of life; for the hills, the plains, and the dales; and for the beauty of meadows and fields, of flowers and of trees.

> *God be praised for the earth.*

For the sky, for the shifting clouds, and for the glory of sunrise and sunset.

> *God be praised for the sky.*

For the sea, that yields and receives again the water without which life would die, and is wonderful in its stillness and more wonderful in its storm.

> *God be praised for the sea.*

For the shelter from wind and weather, which hallowed by love becomes our home; may God strengthen our will that no one shall go hungry or ill-housed or ill-clad.

> *God be praised for our home.*

Let us praise God:

> For our mothers and fathers by whom he orders lives and comforts hearts; may he hallow their work and direct their ways.

> *God be praised for good mothers and fathers.*

For the gift of children; may God help us to train them to be reverent and truthful, that they may gladden our hearts and bring joy to the world.

> *God be praised for children.*

For good friends to rejoice with us in our joys, to cheer us in trouble and to lighten our tasks; may God help us to repay them in fellowship and service.

God be praised for our friends.

Let us praise God:

For joy that heightens all our life and doubles our powers; may God help us to kindle it in the hearts of others.

God be praised for joy.

For mirth, that unites us with others and refreshes us for our work; may God help us to keep it kind and true.

God be praised for mirth.

For health, bringing wholesomeness of body and mind; may God help us to give our strength to his service.

God be praised for health.

Let us praise God for life.

All praise be to God. Amen.

—The Kingdom, the Power, and the Glory

Jesus born in poverty,
     born to bring peace among men,
     workman at Nazareth,

   Have mercy upon us.

Jesus, in whom the proud were scattered and the mighty put
   down,
     giving good things to the hungry,
     exalting them of low degree,

   Have mercy upon us.

Jesus, in whom all the nations of the earth are one,
     in whom is neither bond nor free,
     brother of all,

   Have mercy upon us.

Jesus, preaching good tidings to the poor,
     proclaiming release to the captives,
     setting at liberty them that are bound,

   Have mercy upon us.

Jesus, friend of the poor,
     feeder of the hungry,
     healer of the sick,

   Have mercy upon us.

Jesus, denouncing the oppressor,
     instructing the simple,
     going about to do good,

   Have mercy upon us.

Jesus, teacher of patience,
    pattern of gentleness,
    prophet of the Kingdom of heaven,

>   *Have mercy upon us.*

Jesus, forgiving them that love much,
    drawing all men unto thee,
calling them that labour and are heavy laden,

>   *Have mercy upon us.*

Jesus, who came not to be ministered unto, but to minister,
    who had nowhere to lay thy head,
    loved by the common people,

>   *Have mercy upon us.*

Jesus, betrayed for the sake of money,
    taken by the chief priests,
    condemned by the rulers,

>   *Have mercy upon us.*

Jesus, crucified for us,

>   *Have mercy upon us.*

Jesus, who hast called us to the fellowship of thy Kingdom,
    in whom is no respect of persons,
    who knows us by our fruits,

>   *Have mercy upon us.*

Jesus, who says to us: "Inasmuch as ye have done it unto one
    of the least of these my brethren, ye have done it unto me,"

>   *Have mercy upon us.*

—Percy Dearmer

God, have mercy upon us miserable sinners.

For our ignorance and our greed which have brought multitudes near to starvation in the midst of plenty,

Lord have mercy upon us.

From a sense of our own virtue after giving some slight charity to the needy,

Good Lord, deliver us.

From heedless comfort in the security of our own homes, while families of the poor wander the streets.

Good Lord, deliver us.

From methods of private or public relief which save the body but destroy the spirit; from hurting the finer sensibilities of men and women, robbing them of their pride and self respect,

Good Lord, deliver us.

From false notions that by preaching we can save the souls of men, while unemployment and poverty break their hearts, unbalance their minds, destroy their homes, tempt them beyond measure, visit want and disease upon their children, turn them to bitterness, hatred and rebellion, or to hopelessness, despair, and death,

Good Lord, deliver us.

That our conscience may know no rest until unemployment is abolished,

We beseech thee to hear us, good Lord.

From satisfaction with any revival of trade or renewed prosperity while multitudes can find no work,

Good Lord, deliver us.

That it may please thee to guide us all quickly into that life in which there shall be justice and peace and a sharing of labor, leisure and joy by all peoples of the earth.

We beseech thee to hear us, good Lord. Amen.

—The Witness

A Litany of the Cross

O God of grace and glory, we are the children of sacrifice; our choicest blessings have been bought with the price of blood and tears other than our own;

O Lord, make us thankful.

For all saints and martyrs, prophets and apostles; servants for all of the common good who served you faithfully in scorn of consequence, of whom the world was not worthy,

O Lord, make us thankful.

For the Cross of Christ and his bitter sacrifice; for the truths which there were brought to light, the love unbounded which there was freely given, and the costly salvation which there visited your people,

O Lord, make us thankful.

By his loneliness in the Garden; by his betrayal and trial; by the humiliation of his people's hate, the mockery of his thorny crown, the bitterness of scourging; by the anguish of his Cross; by his unfailing faith in you and love for humankind,

O Lord, make us thankful.

Eternal God, may we, who owe our blessings to so great a cloud of witnesses who have suffered before us, and to Christ whose Cross is our peace, walk as becomes those who are debtors to your grace. From ingratitude, pride and hardness of heart,

>*Good Lord, deliver us.*

Gird us, we pray you, with gratitude and fidelity; devote us to the service of mankind with more zeal; free us from fear, selfishness, and unbelief; thus may we join afresh the company of your servants who in sacrificial living share the fellowship of the Cross of your Son, our Lord and Saviour.

>*Lord, have mercy upon us and grant us this blessing. Amen.*

>—The Riverside Church

A Litany of the Nation

O God, before whom the empires of the past have risen and fallen away, establish this nation in righteousness; and in personal character and public integrity make her foundations sure;

>*Lord, hear our prayer and mercifully bless this people.*

From the ravages of crime, the disgrace of political corruption, and all malicious designs of lawless leaders,

>*Good Lord, deliver us.*

From prejudice of race and color; from all inequity; from loss of liberties bequeathed us by our founders and from careless acceptance of our heritage and neglect of its responsibilities,

Good Lord, deliver us.

From the decline of pure religion, from the failure of moral fibre in our citizenship, from all accounting of things material above virtues spiritual; from vulgarity of life, loss of social conscience, and collapse of national character,

Good Lord, deliver us.

By the faith on which the foundations of our land were laid and by the sacrifices of its pioneers,

We beseech thee to hear us, O Lord.

By the memory of leaders of the nation, whose wisdom has saved us, whose devotion has chastened us, whose characters have inspired us,

We beseech thee to hear us, O Lord.

By the undeserved wealth of our land committed to us and by our trusteeship of power to work weal or woe on the earth,

We beseech thee to hear us, O Lord.

Keep us from pride of mind, and from boasting tongues deliver us; save our national loyalty from narrowness and our flag from shame; by our love for our land may we measure the love of others for their lands, honoring their devotion as we honor our own; and acknowledging thee one God, may we see all peoples as one family and so govern our national affairs that the whole world may become one.

Lord, hear our prayer and mercifully bless this people. Amen.

—The Riverside Church

A Litany of Aspiration

We confess our temptation to measure our lives by the standards of the crowd and to excuse our disordered behavior by appeal to common practices. O Christ, who didst demand of thy disciples "What do ye more than others?" grant us such clarity of vision, independence of mind, and courage of will that we may live according to our best conscience, without fear or favor of the multitude.

We lift up our hearts unto thee, O Lord.

Disturb us with the vision of a just social order. From being contented ourselves while poverty and ignorance, lack of labor, and destitution of soul afflict so many about us,

Good Lord, deliver us.

From complacency with political corruption, racial prejudice, the hardships of unfair industry, the disunion of the church, and the insanity of war,

Good Lord, deliver us.

O God, give us light that we may know the path to walk in. Confirm in us the dreams of seers and the hopes of prophets; let not cynicism blight nor faithlessness uproot our confidence in thy coming kingdom of righteousness upon the earth; and let courage be kindled that we may live as we pray.

Lord, have mercy upon us and grant us this blessing. Amen.

—The Riverside Church

A Litany of Praise

Spirit of God, the fountain of beauty and goodness, from whom eternally stream all things excellent in man and nature, open our eyes to see thy wonder-working in the world and to rejoice in thee.

We praise thee, O Lord.

For the constancy and beauty of thy creation; for the breath of winds, the scent of flowers, the racing clouds, the glory of the trees; for the procession of thy days and nights, the rhythm of thy seasons, and the wonder of thy stars,

We praise thee, O Lord.

For all beauty in human thought and deed, for poet's song and prophet's word, the gift of music and the grace of art; for nobility of character, for the loveliness of friendship, and for the fragrance of souls nourished in thy peace,

We praise thee, O Lord.

Calm our disquieted spirits that they may reflect thy presence in all things excellent and of good report; take thou the dimness of our souls away. Free our hearts from lethargy, our spirits from discouragement, and our lips from complaining, that we may rejoice in thee.

Bless the Lord, O my soul.

For every intimation that we are thy children; for hours of insight when we have clearly seen thy living presence and have been persuaded of thy love; for that we cannot live by bread alone nor find rest until we rest in thee,

Bless the Lord, O my soul.

For all victories of good over evil, wisdom over ignorance, love over hate, we praise thee. For ancient superstitions and ancient oppression done away; for the working of thy purpose in the breaking of bondage, the enlargement of opportunity and the victories of peace,

Bless the Lord, O my soul.

For courage to endure hazard and hardship we praise thee. For teaching us how trials are to be borne and with what answer they are to be beaten back; for courage to face life's adventure; for strength to do what is appointed and for faith to leave the unsolved mysteries in thy care,

Bless the Lord, O my soul.

May all our living speak thy praise. By faithful work and wholesome play, by daily kindliness, by truthfulness of life and tongue, by secret living in thy sight and outward service for the common good,

Bless the Lord, O my soul.

—The Riverside Church

O God who art Love
O God who art Justice
O God who art Pity

Have mercy upon us.

We call thee "Our Father" but deny thee by our divisions of race and class:

Forgive our pretense and hypocrisy, Our Father, and make clean our hearts within us;

For human greed which grasps at greater profits while prices of necessities soar beyond the reach of multitudes:

> *Good Lord, penalize us as thou must until we take the path to greater mutual consideration and concern.*

For the failure to control the national economy in the interest of the general welfare:

> *Renew a right spirit within us, O God, and compel us to mend our ways.*

Save us, we pray, from losing such control of our economic system that multitudes must suffer the shock of being useless and unemployed:

> *We beseech thee to hear us, O Lord.*

That we face ruin unless we change our ways; that we live in a world where to save ourselves we must also save others; that this nation must lead the way toward a better world for all peoples if we ourselves would live:

> *We praise thee, O God. Amen.*

—William Scarlett

Index